Georgia, My State
Habitats

Mountains

by Doraine Bennett

STATE
STANDARDS
PUBLISHING

Your State • Your Standards • Your Grade Level

Dear Educators, Librarians and Parents . . .

Thank you for choosing the *"Georgia, My State"* Series! We have designed this series to support the Georgia Department of Education's Georgia Performance Standards for elementary level Georgia studies. Each book in the series has been written at appropriate grade level as measured by the ATOS Readability Formula for Books (Accelerated Reader), the Lexile Framework for Reading, and the Fountas & Pinnell Benchmark Assessment System for Guided Reading. Photographs and/or illustrations, captions, and other design elements have been included to provide supportive visual messaging to enhance text comprehension. Glossary and Word Index sections introduce key new words and help young readers develop skills in locating and combining information.

We wish you all success in using the *"Georgia, My State"* Series to meet your student or child's learning needs. For additional sources of information, see www.georgiaencyclopedia.org.

Jill Ward, President

Publisher
State Standards Publishing, LLC
1788 Quail Hollow
Hamilton, GA 31811
USA
1.866.740.3056
www.statestandardspublishing.com

Library of Congress Cataloging-in-Publication Data
Bennett, Doraine, 1953-
  Mountains / by Doraine Bennett.
      p. cm. -- (Georgia, my state. Habitats)
  Includes index.
  ISBN-13: 978-1-935077-37-4 (hardcover)
  ISBN-10: 1-935077-37-6 (hardcover)
  ISBN-13: 978-1-935077-42-8 (pbk.)
  ISBN-10: 1-935077-42-2 (pbk.)
  1. Mountain ecology--Georgia--Juvenile literature. 2. Mountain animals--Georgia--Juvenile literature. I. Title.
  QH105.G4B4646 2009
  577.5'309758--dc22
                                        2009012573

Table of Contents

Gray squirrels live in the Mountains habitat.

The Mountains habitat is in north Georgia.

Mountains

Piedmont

Coastal Plain

Marsh and Swamp →

← Coast

Atlantic Ocean

Bears eat yellow jackets like these.

In the Mountains of Georgia

A black bear pushes his long **snout** into a nest of yellow jackets in the forest floor. The snout is his nose. His thick fur protects him from their stings. He snaps his jaws shut and swallows the insects. A noise from a nearby bush alarms the bear. He backs away. But it is only a gray squirrel running through the mountain forest.

These animals live in the Mountains **habitat** of north Georgia. The Mountains habitat provides their food, water, and shelter. A habitat is a place where plants and animals live.

Air rises and cools in the mountains. It rains more here.

Temperatures are colder in the mountains. It snows here, too.

The mountains rise high above sea level.

What is a Mountain Habitat Like?

In the mountains, the land is high above **sea level**. Sea level is the level of land where it meets the ocean. Temperatures are colder at the higher **elevations**. Elevation is the level the land rises above sea level. Plants and animals that need cool weather live in the mountains.

As air rises over the mountains, it cools and releases moisture. So it rains more in the mountains. It snows in the mountains, too.

It's a Fact!

Brasstown Bald is the highest point in Georgia. A person standing on Brasstown Bald is almost a mile higher in elevation than a person standing on the Georgia coast!

One Mile

Trilliums

Mountain laurels and rhododendrons bloom under the trees.

Ferns and Moss

Rhododendron

8

Oak trees need lots of water. They grow well in the mountains.

Trees and Plants of the Georgia Mountains

Hardwood trees like oak and hickory need lots of water. They grow throughout the mountain forests.

The tall trees of the forest provide shelter for smaller plants. Mountain laurels and rhododendrons bloom beneath the trees. They cover the mountainsides. Ferns, moss, and trilliums carpet the forest floor. These plants grow well in the shade of taller trees.

Bears can climb trees in the forest!

Bears also eat insects in dead tree trunks.

Bears eat the plants, berries, and acorns in the mountains. They will eat our food, too!

How Do Bears Live in the Mountains?

Trees and plants provide food for the animals in the Mountains habitat. The black bear eats the stems of young plants. He eats berries and fruit. He eats acorns and nuts. The bear's sharp claws help him tear into dead tree trunks. He eats the insects inside the dead wood. He pushes his long snout into the ground to find roots to eat. His claws are curved. They help the bear climb trees. He climbs trees to reach nuts and fruit.

When people feed bears, they can become dangerous. That is why forest rangers tell us not to feed bears.

BEAR COUNTRY

Store all food in car

All wildlife are dangerous

Snakes hibernate in groups. These garter snakes are coming out of their den!

This bear is awake. He is leaving his den after hibernating.

Raccoons hibernate, too.

Bears hibernate all winter. That's a long time to sleep!

Animal Adaptations

In winter, it is hard for bears to find food. They **hibernate**, or sleep until spring. Their big bodies store energy. They don't need to eat for several months. This is an **adaptation** that helps bears survive. An adaptation is a change an animal or plant makes to survive. The change helps a plant or animal fit better into its **environment**. Environment is the type of conditions a plant, animal, or human lives in.

It's a Fact!

A human heart beats about 70 times each minute. But the black bear's heart rate slows down when he hibernates. It may beat only 8 times each minute!

How many deer are hiding here?

This fawn is following its mother's white tail.

Whitetail deer live in many Georgia habitats.

Animal Camouflage

A whitetail deer and her **fawn** stop to drink at a small stream. A fawn is a young deer. Suddenly, the mother deer lifts her tail and leaps into the forest. The fawn sees the white underside of her tail. It helps the fawn follow her through the trees.

The deer's coat is tan or brown in the summer. It turns gray in winter. Color is the deer's **camouflage**. It hides the deer. She blends into the forest and is hard to see.

American toads have warts on their bodies!

Rainbow trout live in the cool mountain streams.

This brook trout is eating an insect on the water.

Fish and Amphibians in the Mountains

Brook trout and rainbow trout live in the cold mountain streams. The cold water supplies extra oxygen the fish need to survive.

Many types of salamanders live here, too. During the day, the American toad hides under stones or logs near the stream. He hunts for bugs at night. He has warts on his body!

It's a Fact!

The Pigeon Mountain salamander lives only on the eastern slopes of Pigeon Mountain. It is **endemic** to Georgia. It cannot be found anywhere else in the world.

Tennessee

←Lookout Mountain

←Pigeon Mountain

Mountains Habitat

Alabama

Scarlet
Tanager

Ruffed
Grouse

Red-Taile
Hawk

Blue-Winged
Warbler

Pileated woodpeckers peck
for insects to eat.

These wild turkeys are looking for food. Do
they look like your turkey at Thanksgiving

Birds in the Mountains

A family of wild turkeys struts out of the woods. They search for food in a nearby meadow. A pileated woodpecker hammers a tree trunk. It is looking for food to eat. A red-tailed hawk soars overhead. A ruffed grouse builds a nest beneath thick bushes. Some **songbirds** nest in the trees. Songbirds are birds that make musical sounds. The scarlet tanager and the blue-winged warbler are songbirds.

The brown thrasher is a songbird, too. It **thrashes** or moves around in the bushes. It searches through dry leaves to find insects to eat. It is the state bird of Georgia.

Brown Thrasher

The Etowah darter is an endangered species.

The Pigeon Mountain salamander is endangered, too.

Some animals in the Mountains habitat may become extinct like the dinosaurs did.

Protecting the Mountains Habitat

The Georgia State Parks Service helps protect trees and animals in the Mountains habitat. The Parks Service protects other Georgia habitats, too.

Plants and animals can become **extinct** if their habitat is changed. Without food, water, and shelter, they cannot survive.

The Pigeon Mountain salamander is an **endangered species**. It could become extinct. It lives only on Pigeon Mountain in Georgia. The Etowah darter is also endangered. It is a small fish that lives in the Etowah River.

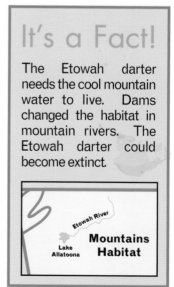

It's a Fact!

The Etowah darter needs the cool mountain water to live. Dams changed the habitat in mountain rivers. The Etowah darter could become extinct.

Etowah River

Lake Allatoona

Mountains Habitat

Glossary

adaptation – A change in behavior that helps a plant or animal fit better into its environment.

camouflage – A way an animal hides by looking like its surroundings.

elevation – The level the land rises above sea level.

endangered species – A group of plants or animals that is in danger of becoming extinct.

endemic – A plant or animal that only lives naturally in a certain area.

environment – The type of conditions a plant, animal, or human lives in.

extinct – A group of plants or animals that has disappeared, or ceased to exist.

fawn – A young deer.

habitat – A place where plants and animals live.

hibernate – To sleep through the winter season, when food is scarce.

sea level – The level of land where it meets the ocean.

snout – The nose of an animal, like a bear.

songbirds – Birds that make musical sounds.

thrashes – The sound a bird or animal makes by moving about in bushes or dry leaves.

Word Index

Image Credits

About the Author

Doraine Bennett has a degree in professional writing from Columbus State University in Columbus, Georgia, and has been writing and teaching writing for over twenty years. She has authored numerous articles in magazines for both children and adults and is the editor of the National Infantry Association's *Infantry Bugler* magazine. Doraine enjoys reading and writing books and articles for children. She lives in Georgia with her husband, Cliff.